Water Colors

Water Colors

Poems by

Barbara Brooks

Cover design by Shay Culligan

ISBN: 978-1-954353-54-1

Kelsay Books
502 South 1040 East, A-119
American Fork, Utah, 84003
Kelsaybooks.com

Acknowledgments

Many thanks to the publications in which versions of the following poems have appeared:

Amarillo Bay: "Red Handled Knife"
Big River Poetry: "Cape Lookout"
Bishop's House Review: "Looking for You at Hansen's Pond," "Turkey Vulture"
Blueline: "The Stream"
Earth's Daughters: "In the Rain"
Green Hills Literary Lantern: "Hunting the Children"
Homestead: "Green"
North Carolina Poetry Society: "Still Life"
Open Minds Quarterly: "Black"
River and Sound: "Black Ornaments"
Rosette Malficarum: "Yellow"
Selcouth Station: "Hurricane Rain at Holden Beach"
Southern Women's Review: "Bluebirds"
Sugar Mule: "After the Rain"
Tar River Poetry: "Black Snake"
Third Wednesday: "Ode to Black," "Coloring Outside the Lines"
Wellspring: "North Pond, Pea Island"
Widow Moon: "Why I Stopped Collecting Shells"

Contents

Green

There are 231 colors of green according to Sherwin-Williams.
I should be able to write a poem about the greens
of the woods and forest floor with this many colors.
Mayapples are their own shade; you know the one I am talking
  about.
The emerging grapevines are covered with a satin finish.
Fiddlehead ferns have several shades; the head is wooly
and darkens as it unfurls to become a jade feather on the woodland
  floor.
Young poison ivy is tinged with a red and glossy finish.
The color of growing maple leaves is as soft as the leaf itself.
Honeysuckle, oak are not among the 231 shades,
but you know the colors I mean.

Looking for You at Hansen's Pond

Fredrica Bishop 1937–2000

I wait for you to guide me
through the wood's greenbrier.

I want to see if today's sky
matches your eyes.

On the pond, the texture
of your paintings glint.

Spring frogs greet me from trees' new growth—
Let others into your life.

Wind riffs my hair—
Float on the breezes.

I stop to listen to your counsel
but hear only pines.

The Stream

Snow laces branches and melts
in the stream that slips
between shaded hills.
Quietly, it slides
past trout lily and snakes
around remnants of shattered
stills. Winding its way
through running cedar,
it passes the ivory
remains of deer season. Snow
softens the landscape
but cannot cover
the bared ribs.

Backyard Stream

Guess you'd call it seasonal, dry
in summer's drought, iced over
in winter, this 150 feet of stream
I own. Last spring, a red-shouldered
hawk hunted in it. He nailed a frog, presented
it to his mate watching from a poplar limb.
Hidden from beneath the bank's overhang,
a blue bird wetted each flight feather,
finished its bath in the redbud.

Yesterday, the brook was a black slash
border lined by snow. Two or three at a time,
goldfinches dipped into an ice-free pool
to drink. Barking up a storm, the dog
pointed to the creek. Cocking its head,
a great blue heron tilts its head,
plodded down the sandbar.

Hunting the Children

Lord of the lagoon,
Great Egret stalks
among the reeds.
Baby duck strays,
huddles between
cattail stems.

Head tilted,
the plumed hunter
snakes forward,
unblinking,
it spears
the duckling,
stilts to dry ground.
From the yellow beak,
webbed feet dangle.

Still Life

I

Feeding,
tipping brown head
beneath the lake's water,
its blue legs pedaling in air,
lone duck.

II

Mallards
idle by river's edge
green-headed male, drab mate.
Brown water ripples their shadow
downstream.

III

Floating
on jade water
amidst feeding birds,
strings of razorbills winging, a
loon wails.

In the Rain

I buried your cat today. Black with white feet, sat
on my porch in the late afternoon sun, stalked the birds from
under the Chinese elm. The one you let roam up and down the
    busy
street. This morning, I found it cold and stiff as the newspaper
    at the end

of the driveway. After work, I went to the barn to see the new
foal, only twelve hours old; his coat melted chocolate and a tiny
white star on his forehead. His legs wobbled as he tried to
walk. It began to rain. He finished nursing, tumbled beneath
his mother's legs to rest,

and I remembered the cat. No one had claimed the damp body. I
dug a shallow grave. The cat was heavy on the end of the shovel.
I covered the body; hoped its death had been quick. I buried
your cat today, and I don't even

know who you are.

Cape Lookout

I sit among dunes, ocean wind
sanding layers of self-doubt:
false accusations,
drinking,
urge to retreat.

Flayed by wind, I move towards shelter
as seafoam skids across the jetty,
purple sandpipers claw to black rocks.
Sand scrapes against my skeletal fears.

Walking towards the sound,
I am punctured by saw palmetto.
Waves clap the shore; I find a wooden jetty,
sit, still the salt burns. I root to the piling.
Low tides bring drying wind.
As the crescent moon rises,
I open to let the high tide feed me.

North Pond, Pea Island

Smooth, cold
a stone skips
the pond's silk.
Riffles weave
outward. Gravity catches
the rock. When it's pulled
to the depths, no circles
mark its passing.

Hurricane Rain at Holden Beach

It slips from the clouds out on the horizon,
marches towards the beach;
great drops pelt the waves with dimples.

It pocks the sand like blasts from a BB gun,
pastes each grain to its neighbor,
sands the driftwood that washes ashore,
rinses dust from the sea oats,
salt from the car pummels the window,
falls softly as the wind drops.

It trickles down my back through the leak
in my raincoat, needles my skin as I lean
into the wind, wishing it would wash
you from my mind.

Why I Stopped Collecting Shells

Jekyll Island is the first beach I remember. I wanted shells that were small, looked like
snails or butterflies. I put them in plastic bags. Mom threw them out; snail shells, it seemed, contained hermit crabs. Older, I returned to the beach. The purest whites, blacks, calico, unblemished—these were the ones I wanted.

The next stage, the perfect shell from each beach I visited: Lion's Paw from the Gulf,
razor clam from the Atlantic. Sand dollars too much to hope for. Stones replaced shells
in the Arctic, the Pacific. The unblemished did not interest. I would rinse the sand off in the pools left by the tide.

Yesterday, I was on a beach full of shells; last night's storm swept it clean. Now I only poke at the shells, maybe pick them up, rub off the sand. I am left to wonder who drilled the holes, what happened to the hermit crab, who ate the tender mussel.

Ocean Scape

I ponder despair and sorrow, wonder the degree
of difference as I watch the waves slap the shore.
Is despair the failure to find the perfect sand dollar
or sorrow the cry of a child when the ocean
takes its sandcastle back to the sea. Or is despair
the undertow pulling me out to the point of no return.

Black Snake

Often it would scare me—draped on the mower handle
or hiding underneath it—sometimes just its skin on the brick wall.

The dog would bark in high alert.
Coiled, it was prepared to strike. With the dog in the house,
I would escort it outside the fence with the rake.

But today, the dog did not bark; only the loud crash
of tubs, buckets, and wood told me something was wrong.
He, shaking the lower half of the torn snake,
danced with pride in the yard.

I searched for the rest of it, mangled in the dirt.
Its ripped lung fluttered like a red flag in the wind.

Ode to Black

A cave's mouth
Swirling bats
Stream smoothed stone
Raven
Onyx
Dog's nose
Chimney swifts spinning into the smokestack.
Sea shell
Vinyl record
Piano's sharps and flats
Burnt candle wick
Horse's mane caught in the wind as he leaves
Lightening scarred tree
The shirt you gave me
Hollow heart

Black Ornaments

adorn the snags: oaks, pines—
vultures rest for the night. In early morning light,
the wind lifts them to scour the roadways
for the frosted carcass. One by one, they drop
from their perch, silver-tipped wings sweep the air.

Every day, hundreds rise to kettle over my head.
I want them to swoop down, land,
pick my brain clean of its black thoughts.

Red Handled Knife

Longer than I have known most of my friends,
I have had that knife. Bought it in Paris.
Small, plastic handle same length as the blade.
We were going to have a wine and cheese party
in the room.

You could take almost anything on the plane
back then, so I packed it in my bag. Since
then, it has followed me to Memphis,
Hillsborough.

Along the way, I must have used it
as a screwdriver, bent the blade.
I cut up hot dogs to hide the greyhound's
thyroid medicine. Still pretty sharp,
except for those dents.

And me? I don't remember the names
of the wine and cheeses. Or if we had bread.
Can't recall a single face of the people
I shared it with. Rarely think of Paris,
if at all.

Blue Leash

Patterned with bones and hearts, I hook
it to George's collar and think back
to when I got Hannah, who sat confused
and crying in the car. My brother sent
it to me when I got her: *for your new dog.*
The matching collar sits on the mantel
along with her paw print, picture, and ashes.

Shades of Gray

The trees are silvered with ice,
limbs droop, unable to hold
the weight. Some have snapped;
pine sap scents the air
against the backdrop of slate.
The branches sway in the wind
against smoky sky.
Pop, crash, a leaden branch snags
the wires and they bounce in their coats
of ice. The house is quiet, no refrigerator
humming, no heat pump compressor.
The weak sun tries to pierce
the pewter clouds,
makes only enough light to read
by the window.

Bluebirds

The male, azure with cinnamon vest, points the way
to an abandoned woodpecker hole. The female weaves
a nest of pine needles, grass. The young,
naked, blind, demand food.

> *In the next room, the baby cries:*
> *Wet diaper.*

Green worm in his bill, he waits in a nearby tree,
searches for danger, enters the hole. He leaves, carries
a fecal sac from the nest.

> *The father turns up the volume.*

The black snake shimmies up the tree,
parents peck and fuss; chickadees, nuthatches mob it.
Defeated, the snake retreats.

> *Shut that baby up.*
> *She rouses from the couch.*
> *I'll give him something to cry about.*

Feathered and sighted, the fledglings
peer from the hole. The father calls to the young: fly.

> *the water, hot*

The female starts another nest.

> *the child screams.*

Black

Against the snow, the Angus bull
        looks like a prize winner,
                shoulders muscled, blacker
than black.
        Floating on wind current,
                vultures are black
streamers. Around
        dead deer, a moving sack
                of black rags. Forest dark
becomes light
        when the scraper blade slices
                a new driveway and backhoe
punctures the clay for foundation.

        In my hand, the pills look like sprinkles
                on an ice cream sundae,
green, yellow, red. Bottom
        of the glass, I see
            black.

Pond

Bronzes and rubies whisper,
drop onto the gold dish,
trapped in the riffles

from dead branches. Along
the surface, frozen leaves' veins
rupture and begin

to leak amber. Water
distills into whisky brown
like the drink I want.

Turkey Vulture

The black wing
    scythes the thermal
        falling lower or rising

higher on the turn
    of a feather.
        Swooping low,

the bird scans the earth
    for the dead
        or the solitary.

Vulture, knife down,
    probe deep, cut
        these memories

so I can slice
        the wind.

Coloring Outside the Lines

The sky darkens to the ace of spades.
He drinks coffee, thick as tar,
while the tires whine on the road,
headlights carve a light
into the cave of a country night.

Tomorrow is the funeral; her bruises will be covered
by mortician's powder. He can't find the flower
of her favorite color; it doesn't exist. Dark purple roses
will have to grace her coffin. The thunderheads will blossom
and spill rain on the raven sitting on the steeple.

After the Rain

Stream flows, not quite out of its banks.
Titmouse calls, an echo.
Birch leaf, white flag of winter's surrender,
flutters to ground.
Spider floats silk between trees.
Rain drops jewel redbud.

Squirrel breakfasts on seeds,
starts a nest. Cuts and balances a twig,
maneuvers it to the crotch of sycamore.
Takes a break, inspects a hole in dead snag,
leaps to maple only to disappear.

Wind tears through greening tulip poplar,
rips tender leaf from branch.
Worm dries in sun, rain-driven
from soil. Ferns unravel by rotting log.
May apples umbrella forest floor.

Yellow

Fireflies hide on stems
of unmown grass,
wait for dusk. The falling sun
pulls them up. Five, six, ten lift
themselves three,
four, twelve feet into the trees.
Their abdomens flash
yellow, their wings blur.

In the still morning, tiger
swallowtails drop from underneath
green leaves. They tease nectar
from the buddleia. Unheard,
their wings flutter as they
wander. Like boxers, two spar
upward. Like Japanese
lanterns, ten now twenty
hang from purple flowers.

About the Author

Barbara is a retired physical therapist living in North Carolina and a member of the poetry group Poet Fools. She is an avid birder and has traveled extensively throughout the world, viewing wild birds in their natural habitat. She frequently incorporates nature in her poetry as an extension of her love of the outdoors. She has two chapbooks: *The Catbird Sang* and *A Shell to Return to the Sea.* She has had published poems in a number of eclectic journals such as *Jellyfish Whispers, Tar River Poetry, Peregrine,* and *Third Wednesday.*

www.ingramcontent.com/pod-product-compliance
Lightning Source LLC
Chambersburg PA
CBHW031155090426
42738CB00008B/1348